TOP TRUMPS®

ULTIMATE CARS

D1381639

© **Haynes Publishing 2006**

All rights reserved. No part of this publication may be reproduced or
transmitted in any form or by any means, electronic or mechanical,
including photocopying, recording or by any information storage or
retrieval system, without permission in writing from Haynes Publishing.

This book is officially licensed by Winning Moves UK Ltd,
owners of the Top Trumps registered trademark.

Matt Saunders has asserted his right to be identified as the
author of this book.

British Library Cataloguing-in-Publication Data:
A catalogue record for this book is available from the British Library

ISBN 1 84425 395 3

Library of Congress catalog card no. 2006928054

Published by Haynes Publishing,
Sparkford, Yeovil, Somerset BA22 7JJ, UK
Tel: 01963 442030 Fax: 01963 440001
Int. tel: +44 1963 442030 Int. fax: +44 1963 440001
Email: sales@haynes.co.uk
Website: www.haynes.co.uk

Haynes North America, Inc.,
861 Lawrence Drive, Newbury Park
California 91320, USA

Printed and bound in Great Britain by
J. H. Haynes & Co. Ltd, Sparkford

Photographic credits:
Neill Bruce: Ferrari F40, Jaguar XJ220
Kent Churchill: Pontiac GTO
Tim Cottingham: Aston Martin DB4 GT Zagato
Chr. Gonzenbach © Neill Bruce: Ferrari Enzo
LAT Photographic: Audi Quattro, Ferrari 250 GTO, Honda NSX-R, Lotus
Esprit, Maserati Bora, McLaren F1, Porsche 959, Subaru Impreza
Rinsey Mills: AC Cobra

The Author

Matt Saunders is Features Editor for *Autocar*, the world's oldest car
magazine, where he has worked since 2003. Prior to that, he was a staff
writer and motoring specialist on *Stuff* magazine.

TOP TRUMPS®

ULTIMATE CARS

Contents

POWER BY COSWORTH

About
Top Trumps

It's now more than 30 years since Britain's kids first caught the Top Trumps craze. The game remained hugely popular until the 1990s, when it slowly drifted into obscurity. Then, in 1999, UK games company Winning Moves discovered it, bought it, dusted it down, gave it a thorough makeover and introduced it to a whole new generation. And so the Top Trumps legend continues.

Nowadays, there are Top Trumps titles for just about everyone, with subjects about animals, cars, ships, aircraft and all the great films and TV shows. Top Trumps is now even more popular than before. In Britain, a pack of Top Trumps is bought every six seconds! And it's not just British children who love the game. Children in Australasia, the Far East, the Middle East, all over Europe and in North America can buy Top Trumps at their local shops.

Today you can even play the game on the internet, interactive DVD, your games console and even your mobile phone.

You've played the game...

Now read the book

Haynes Publishing and Top Trumps have teamed up to bring you this exciting new Top Trumps book, in which you will find even more pictures, details and statistics.

Top Trumps: Ultimate Cars features 45 of the world's most exciting road cars, ranging from the sensational F1-inspired Ferrari Enzo to the exotic Pagani Zonda F and the monstrous Bugatti Veyron. Packed with fascinating facts, stunning photographs and all the vital statistics, this is the essential pocket guide. And if you're lucky enough to spot any of these ultimate cars, then at the back of the book we've provided space for you to record when and where you saw them.

Look out for other Top Trumps books from Haynes Publishing
even more facts, even more fun!

AC Cobra
289

A snake with a venomous bite

FYW 96C

FYW 96C

AC Cobra
289

A snake with a venomous bite

When Britain and America team up, great things can happen; look to the AC Cobra for proof of that. The Cobra was the brainchild of US entrepreneur Carroll Shelby. In 1961, he approached British sports car maker AC with a pioneering idea; why not take its finest sports car, a lightweight roadster called the Ace, and fit it with one of the world's greatest engines – Ford's 4.7-litre, 300bhp V8? The results stunned the car-loving world. The original Cobra could get to 60mph in less than six seconds and go on to 140mph. Today, 45 years later, the very fastest new hatchbacks couldn't keep up. Yet the Cobra would just go on getting faster. By the end of its life it had a monstrous 7.0-litres and 400bhp to call upon to match its notoriously sideways handling manners. If you can tame a Cobra, there really isn't anything else on four wheels to be afraid of. There's no other car in the world more aptly named either.

Statistics

Price	£2732
0-60mph:	5.5sec
0-100mph:	13.5sec
Max speed:	140mph (225kph)
Engine type:	8 cylinders in a V
Engine capacity:	4727cc
Bore x stroke:	101.6mm x 72.9mm
Max power:	300bhp @ 5750rpm
Max torque:	285lb ft @ 4500rpm
Power to weight ratio:	286bhp per tonne
Transmission:	four-speed manual gearbox, rear-wheel drive
Kerb weight:	1050kg
Length:	4020mm
Width:	1600mm
Height:	1220mm
Fuel consumption:	15.1mpg
Year introduced:	1962

FYW 96C

Ariel Atom
300
Don't forget your helmet

Ariel Atom
300
Don't forget your helmet

When you get down to it, supercar-making is driven by the sciences of power and weight so, if you want to judge roughly how fast a car is, the power-to-weight ratio is the best place to start. The fastest road car featured on these pages, the Bugatti Veyron, musters 523bhp for every tonne it weighs; this one, however, manages an even more amazing 652bhp per tonne. That's because the Atom's 300 horsepower supercharged Honda VTEC engine is seated inside an aluminium body that tips the scales at just 460kg without any fuel on board. There are motorbikes that weigh almost as much as that. Built without a windscreen, a roof, doors or even body panels, this flyweight four-wheeler is all about uncompromised speed, and on a perfectly dry circuit only a very skilled driver, at the wheel of one of only a handful of super-quick cars, would stand a chance of even seeing which way it went.

Statistics

Price	£35,000
0-60mph:	2.0sec
0-100mph:	6.8sec
Max speed:	151mph (242kph)
Engine type:	4 cylinders in line, supercharged
Engine capacity:	1998cc
Bore x stroke:	86mm x 86mm
Max power:	300bhp @ 8200rpm
Max torque:	191lb ft @ 7150rpm
Power to weight ratio:	652bhp per tonne
Transmission:	six-speed close ratio manual gearbox, rear-wheel drive
Kerb weight:	460kg
Length:	3410mm
Width:	1798mm
Height:	1195mm
Fuel consumption:	n/a
Year introduced:	2004

Aston Martin DB4 GT
Zagato

Grace and pace in one beautiful place

FLEMINGS

73 GYL

Aston Martin DB4 GT
Zagato

Grace and pace in one beautiful place

The trouble with beauty is that it's subjective; one man's Mona Lisa is another's Waynetta Slob. However, of all the cars you'll find on these pages, this is the one most likely to have you swooning in your cornflakes; the Aston Martin DB4 GT Zagato – more lovely, many would argue, than the Jaguar E-type, the Citroën DS or the Lamborghini Miura. Unlike those three cars, this DB4's beauty was borne out of the need for speed. At the end of the 1950s, Aston Martin and Ferrari were bitter racing rivals and, unfortunately for Aston, its DB4 GTs were being made to look slow by the unstoppable Ferrari 250 GTs. In an attempt to find some speed, Aston recruited Italian stylists Zagato to produce a lighter, more aerodynamic body for its racer. This dropdead gorgeous GT is what Zagato came up with – a sleek fusion of handsome British design and delicate Italian styling. Only 19 were made, every one still exists and each is now worth a cool £1.6million. And what wouldn't you give to have one on your driveway?

Statistics

Price	£5469
0-60mph:	6.1sec
0-100mph:	14.1sec
Max speed:	154mph (247kph)
Engine type:	6 cylinders in line
Engine capacity:	3670cc
Bore x stroke:	92mm x 92mm
Max power:	314bhp @ 6000rpm
Max torque:	278lb ft @ 5400rpm
Power to weight ratio:	251bhp per tonne
Transmission:	four-speed manual gearbox, rear-wheel drive
Kerb weight:	1251kg
Length:	4270mm
Width:	1670mm
Height:	1280mm
Fuel consumption:	13.9mpg
Year introduced:	1960

Aston Martin
Vanquish S

The very best of British

Aston Martin
Vanquish S

The very best of British

It takes something very special indeed to beat the most desirable supercars in the world at their own game. That's exactly what the Aston Martin Vanquish did. The Vanquish was Aston's attempt to get serious; it was blue-blooded, V12-engined, and staggeringly beautiful, and was aimed directly at the best that the likes of Ferrari and Lamborghini could produce. It was also a film star, of course; the car that lured James Bond back from the trio of German BMWs he'd driven during the 90s, into something that better reflected his fiery Anglo Saxon temperament. Aston refined the Vanquish recipe in 2004, boosting its engine power from 460 to 520bhp, stiffening its suspension, quickening its steering, and giving it even bigger brakes. In doing that, it gave birth to the first ever 200mph Aston road car, and turned what was already a great into a world-beater. But then, as 007 drives one, wouldn't it have to be good enough to take on the world and win?

Statistics

Price	**£174,000**
0-60mph:	**4.8sec**
0-100mph:	**10.1sec**
Max speed:	**201mph (322kph)**
Engine type:	**12 cylinders in a V**
Engine capacity:	**5935cc**
Bore x stroke:	**89mm x 79.5mm**
Max power:	**520bhp @ 7000rpm**
Max torque:	**425lb ft @ 5800rpm**
Power to weight ratio:	**277bhp per tonne**
Transmission:	**six-speed paddleshift gearbox, rear-wheel drive**
Kerb weight:	**1875kg**
Length:	**4665mm**
Width:	**1923mm**
Height:	**1318mm**
Fuel consumption:	**13.4mpg**
Year introduced:	**2004**

Audi
Quattro

The first fast 4x4

Audi quattro 20V

Audi
Quattro
The first fast 4x4

Audi quattro 20V

Don't let anyone tell you that four-wheel-drives belong only in fields. It's not just Land Rovers that use all four wheels to move forward; today, there's an entire breed of performance cars that rely on four-wheel drive to grab the tarmac underneath them and throw them down the road. This, however, was the first – Audi's magnificent Quattro. In the late 1970s, Audi was a struggling arm of German car-maker Volkswagen; the Quattro, which arrived in 1980, was the car that transformed its fortunes. It was a two-door coupé adapted from the company's compact saloon, the 80. What made it unique was that its turbocharged engine sent power to all four of its wheels. It was a hugely successful formula; the Quattro could go fast in any weather, sold all over the world and swept the board in the World Rally Championship two years running. Without it, there'd be no Lancia Delta Integrale, no Subaru Impreza and no Mitsubishi Lancer Evolution; the Quattro's a legend.

Statistics

Price	**£14,500**
0-60mph:	**7.3sec**
0-100mph:	**20.7sec**
Max speed:	**137mph (220kph)**
Engine type:	**5 cylinders in line, turbocharged**
Engine capacity:	**2214cc**
Bore x stroke:	**79.5mm x 86.4mm**
Max power:	**200bhp @ 5500rpm**
Max torque:	**210lb ft @ 3500rpm**
Power to weight ratio:	**158bhp per tonne**
Transmission:	**five-speed manual gearbox, four-wheel drive**
Kerb weight:	**1264kg**
Length:	**4404mm**
Width:	**1723mm**
Height:	**1344mm**
Fuel consumption:	**19.1mpg**
Year introduced:	**1980**

Audi
R8

The Lamborghini from Germany

Audi
R8

The Lamborghini from Germany

A new power is rising in supercar land, in the shape of a car company that has hitherto stuck to making more ordinary cars, but that is now shooting for the stars. Meet the R8 – the car that, Audi hopes, can capitalise on the success it has enjoyed in great sports car races like Le Mans and Sebring in recent years, and can tempt you out of your Ferrari, Porsche or Aston Martin. Every last bit of knowledge that Audi has about making fast cars has gone into this car; it is built almost completely of lightweight aluminium instead of steel, has Quattro four-wheel drive and an engine mounted behind the driver but between the front and rear axles for peerless cornering dynamics. That engine isn't any ordinary motor either, but the 480bhp 5.0-litre V10 screamer from the Lamborghini Gallardo – the Italian supercar company that Audi bought in 1998. Be afraid, Ferrari; you have been warned.

Price	**£100,000***
0-60mph:	**4.0sec***
0-100mph:	**9.5sec***
Max speed:	**200mph (320kph)***
Engine type:	**10 cylinders in a V**
Engine capacity:	**4961cc**
Bore x stroke:	**82.5mm x 92.8mm**
Max power:	**480bhp @ 8000rpm***
Max torque:	**360lb ft @ 4500rpm***
Power to weight ratio:	**331bhp per tonne***
Transmission:	**six-speed paddleshift gearbox, four-wheel drive**
Kerb weight:	**1450kg***
Length:	**4370mm**
Width:	**1900mm**
Height:	**1250mm**
Fuel consumption:	**15mpg***
Year introduced:	**2007**

* figures are estimates based on latest information

Audi
RS4
A hundred horsepower per corner

Audi
RS4
A hundred horsepower per corner

Some cars are born great; they're intended to achieve the extraordinary right from the first stroke of the designer's pencil. Others, however, have greatness thrust upon them later in life, and the Audi RS4 is a car from the second of those camps. The basics of its design are the same as any other Audi A4 – a fairly ordinary family saloon of the kind that you see on the motorway every few moments. Like the A4, it has four doors, a roomy cabin to sit in, a decent-sized boot at the back and an engine up front. It's the specifics that make the RS4 special. In place of, say, a 130 horsepower 2.0-litre engine, this saloon car has 4.2-litres of V8 craziness, which revs all the way to 8250rpm, and delivers a massive 414bhp – more than any other four-door of its size. Being an Audi, it sends that power to all four wheels too, making it the most awesome all-weather super saloon in the business.

Statistics

Price	£49,980
0-60mph:	4.5sec
0-100mph:	10.5sec
Max speed:	163mph (262kph)
Engine type:	8 cylinders in a V
Engine capacity:	4163cc
Bore x stroke:	84.5mm x 92.8mm
Max power:	414bhp @ 7800rpm
Max torque:	317lb ft @ 5500rpm
Power to weight ratio:	251bhp per tonne
Transmission:	six-speed manual gearbox, four-wheel drive
Kerb weight:	1650kg
Length:	4585mm
Width:	1935mm
Height:	1415mm
Fuel consumption:	20.9mpg
Year introduced:	2006

BMW
M3 CSL

The drifter's dream car

BMW
M3 CSL

The drifter's dream car

The BMW M3 is 20 this year. Over that time, this compact two-door coupé has become one of the most respected sports cars there is, thanks to a recipe that includes lots of power, entertaining handling, surprising practicality and muscular but understated looks. Its story starts in the cauldron of motorsport. The first, 1986 M3 was built and sold in tiny numbers, in order that BMW could take it racing in the European touring car championship. However, such was its popularity that BMW has since sold M3s in their hundreds of thousands. The fastest and most hardcore version of the car is known as the M3 CSL and, in this form, the car had been honed into one of the most delicately balanced and fun-to-drive coupés ever made. Also, with 360bhp, rear-wheel drive and a fast-acting differential, it's one of the best cars on the road in which to learn to powerslide. Want to grow up to be a world drifting champion? Then this is the car you need.

Statistics

Price	£58,455
0-60mph:	4.8sec
0-100mph:	10.9sec
Max speed:	156mph (250kph)
Engine type:	6 cylinders in a line
Engine capacity:	3246cc
Bore x stroke:	87mm x 91mm
Max power:	360bhp @ 7900rpm
Max torque:	273lb ft @ 4900rpm
Power to weight ratio:	260bhp per tonne
Transmission:	six-speed paddleshift gearbox, rear-wheel drive
Kerb weight:	1385kg
Length:	4492mm
Width:	1780mm
Height:	1365mm
Fuel consumption:	23.7mpg
Year introduced:	2003

BMW
M5
Powered by Formula 1

How great would it be, ask yourself, to drive around in a car powered by an engine directly related to that of a Formula 1 racing car? Imagine exploding away from traffic lights with a howl so alike to Juan Pablo Montoya's 2004 Williams F1 car that you'd swear he was only three car-lengths behind you. That's what driving BMW's M5 is like. The V10 engine in this saloon car is made in the same factory as the V10 engines that, until only this season, powered the Williams F1 team. It's one of the most sophisticated motors ever offered in a road car, and gives the M5 a full 500bhp – which is more power, incidentally, than a Ferrari F430. The M5 is also fitted with a seven-speed paddleshift gearbox that can change gear in just 50 milliseconds and, if it weren't electronically limited to 155mph, would hit 205mph in a straight line. It's not quite the fastest four-door money can buy, then – but it's definitely the most technically advanced.

Statistics

Price	£63,495
0-60mph:	4.7sec
0-100mph:	9.7sec
Max speed:	156mph (250kph)
Engine type:	10 cylinders in a V
Engine capacity:	4999cc
Bore x stroke:	92mm x 75.2mm
Max power:	500bhp @ 7750rpm
Max torque:	383lb ft @ 6100rpm
Power to weight ratio:	277bhp per tonne
Transmission:	seven-speed paddleshift gearbox, rear-wheel drive
Kerb weight:	1830kg
Length:	4855mm
Width:	2050mm
Height:	1469mm
Fuel consumption:	14.5mpg
Year introduced:	2004

Brabus
Rocket

Four doors, absolutely no waiting

Brabus
Rocket

Four doors, absolutely no waiting

Brabus is a German tuning company that turns quite ordinary Mercedes into some of the most monstrously powerful cars on the road and, as an outfit, it isn't known for doing things by halves. It might surprise you to find out that the fastest saloon car on the planet (a saloon has, by definition, four doors and four seats) isn't made by Audi, BMW or Porsche – it's this, the Brabus Rocket. And boy, does it fly, hitting 62mph in just 4.0 seconds, 125mph in 10.5 seconds, and not stopping piling on the speed until 220mph. The car is based on a Mercedes-Benz CLS, but underneath the skin it's rather different to Mercedes' stock four-seater. Brabus has tweaked the air suspension, fitted lightweight alloys wheels, special tyres and powerful carbon-ceramic brakes. Under the bonnet is where the car's real genius lies though; here, you'll find a 6.2-litre twin-turbocharged V12 tuned to deliver 720bhp and a mighty 812lb ft of torque. If you see one parked by the side of the road then you'd be well advised to get in, or get out of its way.

Statistics

Price	£275,000
0-60mph:	4.0sec
0-100mph:	8.5sec
Max speed:	220mph (349kph)
Engine type:	12 cylinders in a V, twin turbocharged
Engine capacity:	6233cc
Bore x stroke:	85.5mm x 87.5mm
Max power:	720bhp @ 5100rpm
Max torque:	812lb ft @ 2100rpm
Power to weight ratio:	364bhp per tonne
Transmission:	five-speed auto' gearbox, rear-wheel drive
Kerb weight:	1980kg
Length:	4915mm
Width:	1873mm
Height:	1389mm
Fuel consumption:	12mpg
Year introduced:	2004

Bugatti
Veyron 16.4

The fastest of the fast

Bugatti
Veyron 16.4
The fastest of the fast

A 252mph top speed is fast – so fast that it's almost impossible to imagine what it must feel like. It's faster than the fastest living animal (the Peregrine Falcon, which can dive at up to 200mph), faster than the take-off speed of a Eurofighter Typhoon (180mph), faster even than a Formula One racing car. Under the engine cover of this monster you'll find a gigantic 8.0-litre motor with four turbochargers, producing no less than 987bhp – ten times as much power as an average family car. It has seven forward gears, four-wheel drive, can get to 100mph from a standstill before most cars even get to 50mph, and costs nearly £900,000. It's probably the world's fastest new car, and also the most expensive and exclusive. For straight line speed, there has never been another car like the Veyron, and there may very well never be ever again. No other road car ever built even stands a chance of keeping up.

Statistics

Price	£891,000
0-60mph:	2.8sec
0-100mph:	5.5sec
Max speed:	252mph (406kph)
Engine type:	16 cylinders in a 'W', four turbochargers
Engine capacity:	7993cc
Bore x stroke:	86mm x 86mm
Max power:	987bhp @ 6000rpm
Max torque:	922lb ft @ 3500rpm
Power to weight ratio:	523bhp per tonne
Transmission:	seven-speed paddleshift gearbox, four-wheel drive
Kerb weight:	1888kg
Length:	4462mm
Width:	1998mm
Height:	1204mm
Fuel consumption:	11.7mpg
Year introduced:	2005

Caterham
CSR 260

Nearly 50 and quicker than ever

Caterham
CSR 260

Nearly 50 and quicker than ever

We've no wish to confuse you here, but the Caterham you're looking at is actually a Lotus. Lotus founder Colin Chapman designed this car fifty years ago. Back then, it was known as the Lotus Seven; today, after a small British kit car company bought the rights to the car from Lotus in 1973, we know it as the Caterham Seven and, despite the age of its design and the oldie-worldie looks, it remains one of the very fastest cars you can buy. This particular one, in fact, is the latest in a long line of unbelievably quick Caterhams, and it's called the CSR 260. It has a much more sophisticated suspension system and a much more modern cabin than any Seven that's gone before. There's also a boisterious 2.3-litre four cylinder engine hidden away within that stubby snout, which serves up 260bhp and 200lb ft of torque – enough, in a car so small and light, to give an Ariel Atom a run for its money on the track.

Statistics

Price	£37,000
0-60mph:	3.2sec
0-100mph:	7.6sec
Max speed:	143mph (230kph)
Engine type:	4 cylinders in a line
Engine capacity:	2261cc
Bore x stroke:	87.5mm x 94mm
Max power:	260bhp @ 7500rpm
Max torque:	200lb ft @ 6000rpm
Power to weight ratio:	456bhp per tonne
Transmission:	six-speed manual gearbox, rear-wheel drive
Kerb weight:	570kg
Length:	3300mm
Width:	1685mm
Height:	1092mm
Fuel consumption:	24.0mpg
Year introduced:	2005

Chevrolet Corvette
Z06

America's new superpower

79 M491

Chevrolet Corvette
ZO6

America's new superpower

The Chevrolet Corvette is America's own, true blue, home grown sports car. It was also America's first, appearing in 1953, and pre-dating US motoring institutions such as the Ford Mustang and Pontiac GTO, as well as Britain's own Jaguar E-type. But the 'Vette has come a long way since then – and here's the proof. The Corvette ZO6 is the fastest and most powerful Corvette ever. It has enjoyed huge success in the world FIA GT racing championships, and now Chevrolet is selling road-going models, built from a mixture of lightweight aluminium, magnesium, steel and carbon fibre, all over Europe. At the heart of any 'Vette there has to be a throbbing V8 engine and the ZO6's really is something very special. Standard Corvettes get a 6.0-litre V8; the ZO6, however, has 7.0-litres 'under the hood', which makes 506bhp and 475lb ft of torque – suitably epic outputs for a car with such a long and celebrated past.

Statistics

Price	£59,995
0-60mph:	3.9sec
0-100mph:	8.5sec
Max speed:	200mph (320kph)
Engine type:	8 cylinders in a V
Engine capacity:	7008cc
Bore x stroke:	101.6mm x 92mm
Max power:	506bhp @ 6200rpm
Max torque:	475lb ft @ 4800rpm
Power to weight ratio:	357bhp per tonne
Transmission:	six-speed manual gearbox, rear-wheel drive
Kerb weight:	1418kg
Length:	4460mm
Width:	1928mm
Height:	1244mm
Fuel consumption:	19.2mpg
Year introduced:	2006

Ferrari
250 GTO

Supercar number one

Ferrari
250 GTO

Supercar number one

You're looking at the first ever supercar – the Ferrari 250 GTO.
The way this car was built, the ingredients that went into it, and
the way it performed set a pattern that has been followed by
every other supercar-maker since. The 250 GTO came along
in 1962, two years before the Ford GT40 and four years ahead
of the Lamborghini Miura. It was the first proper dual-purpose
performance car, designed to be driven to the track, raced around
it, and then driven home. It was also one of the first performance
cars whose shape was honed in a wind tunnel, and featured a
venomous V12 engine, disc brakes instead of drums and a cabin
that was stripped down to the bare minimum. The 250 GTO has
everything; it was fast (capable of 150mph), won races (three
international GT championship wins), and was very rare (only
39 were ever built). Today, there's no more clearer indicator of
its renown than the fact that genuine examples sell for around
£5,000,000. Makes a Veyron look pretty cheap, doesn't it?

Statistics

Price	£6500
0-60mph:	5.0sec
0-100mph:	11.0sec
Max speed:	150mph (240kph)
Engine type:	12 cylinders in a V
Engine capacity:	2953cc
Bore x stroke:	73mm x 58.8mm
Max power:	300bhp @ 8000rpm
Max torque:	250lb ft @ 7500rpm
Power to weight ratio:	267bhp per tonne
Transmission:	five-speed manual gearbox, rear-wheel drive
Kerb weight:	1125kg
Length:	4400mm
Width:	1675mm
Height:	1245mm
Fuel consumption:	18mpg
Year introduced:	1962

Ferrari
Enzo

The great man's greatest yet

Ferrari
Enzo

The great man's greatest yet

Being able to justifiably lay claim to the title of greatest Ferrari ever is no mean achievement. Doing so makes the Enzo greater than the successful 250, the beautiful 288, even the awesome F40. However, if you experienced the Enzo – if you felt the potency of its acceleration, the unerring composure of its handling, and the savagery of its brakes for yourself – trust us, you'd struggle to disagree. If you look at the statistics, you could be deceived into thinking that the Enzo was unexceptional; don't be. This car will beat a McLaren F1 to 125mph. Its body is made almost exclusively of feather-light carbon fibre. The reason that it looks like it should be lined up on a Formula 1 grid is because every surface on its body is shaped to push against the passing airflow and keep the Enzo stuck to the tarmac. You're looking, essentially, at a fighter jet without wings. Now which way's the racetrack?

Price	**£425,000**
0-60mph:	**3.5sec**
0-100mph:	**6.7sec**
Max speed:	**218mph (349kph)**
Engine type:	**12 cylinders in a V**
Engine capacity:	**5998cc**
Bore x stroke:	**92mm x 75.2mm**
Max power:	**650bhp @ 7800rpm**
Max torque:	**485lb ft @ 5500rpm**
Power to weight ratio:	**476bhp per tonne**
Transmission:	**six-speed paddleshift gearbox, rear-wheel drive**
Kerb weight:	**1365kg**
Length:	**4702mm**
Width:	**2035mm**
Height:	**1147mm**
Fuel consumption:	**12.3mpg**
Year introduced:	**2002**

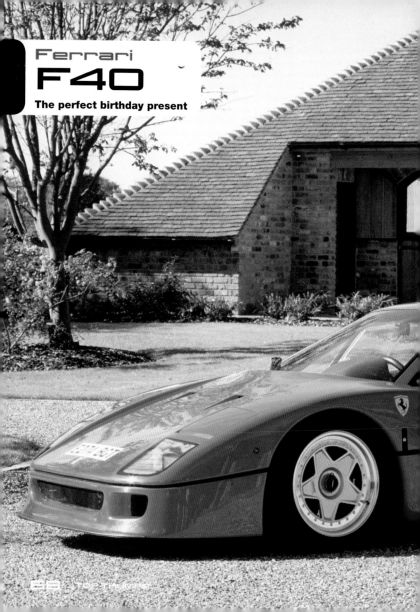

Ferrari
F40

The perfect birthday present

Ferrari
F40

The perfect birthday present

For a generation of schoolboys, the Ferrari F40 occupied an unrivalled position on bedroom walls, and doodled in exercise books. It was the supercar we drove in our dreams, and remains the most evocative Ferrari ever – the shape that visualises the word 'supercar' better than any other. So called because it marked the 40th anniversary of the company in 1987, the F40 was designed for the road, not the track. For that reason, it feels less aggressive to drive than many other supercars; it has adjustable rear suspension to allow the driver to tailor the way it handles to suit the road he's on, and not one, but two fuel tanks. The F40 isn't short on speed; its twin-turbocharged V8 engine produces 478bhp, sends it to a maximum 202mph, and gives the F40 the kind of power delivery that demands your full attention. But it's not the performance itself, but the way that performance is delivered, that's why the F40 is so highly regarded. Some of us still dream about it.

Statistics

Price	£165,000
0-60mph:	3.8sec
0-100mph:	7.7sec
Max speed:	203mph (325kph)
Engine type:	8 cylinders in a V, twin turbocharged
Engine capacity:	2936cc
Bore x stroke:	82mm x 69.5mm
Max power:	478bhp @ 7800rpm
Max torque:	426lb ft @ 4000rpm
Power to weight ratio:	435bhp per tonne
Transmission:	five-speed manual gearbox, rear-wheel drive
Kerb weight:	1100kg
Length:	4430mm
Width:	1980mm
Height:	1130mm
Fuel consumption:	17mpg
Year introduced:	1987

E274 BGT

Ford
Focus RS

Hot hatchback heaven

Ford
Focus RS

Hot hatchback heaven

RS02 HOT

How could you count a Ford Focus, still the most common new car in the UK, alongside a Ferrari Enzo, a McLaren F1 and a Lamborghini Murcielago in a list of the best performance cars ever created? Because this particular Ford Focus is the best hot hatchback there has ever been; better than the current Focus ST, the frantic Honda Civic Type-R – even the original, mould-making 1977 Volkswagen Golf GTI. No other manufacturer has ever crammed in so much rally-bred equipment as Ford did in 2002, when it turned this once-humble family runaround into an unforgettable driver's car. The Focus RS has scooped Sparco bucket seats, a hard, race-car like ride, a 212bhp turbocharged four-cylinder engine, a special Quaife differential metering out the power to the front wheels – and absolutely no electronic traction control. It's the only hot hatchback that feels like a racing car to drive, the only one that's just as at home at a trackday as it is in the supermarket car park.

Statistics

Price	£19,995
0-60mph:	6.3sec
0-100mph:	16.4sec
Max speed:	143mph (230kph)
Engine type:	4 cylinders in a line, turbocharged
Engine capacity:	1998cc
Bore x stroke:	84.8mm x 88mm
Max power:	212bhp @ 5500rpm
Max torque:	229lb ft @ 3500rpm
Power to weight ratio:	166bhp per tonne
Transmission:	five-speed manual gearbox, front-wheel drive
Kerb weight:	1278kg
Length:	4183mm
Width:	1998mm
Height:	1460mm
Fuel consumption:	22mpg
Year introduced:	2002

Ford
GT
A racing icon reborn

Ford GT

A racing icon reborn

EU 04 CWV

Back in the 60s, it took a car company as large as Ford to break Ferrari's six-year dominance of the Le Mans 24hrs, and a supercar as brutally fast as the Ford GT40. This was a supercar for the common man, and proof that you don't need an exotic name or a long racing history to win the biggest race of them all. The GT40 won at Le Mans four years on the trot, between 1966 and 1969; it became an automotive icon. And just three years ago, Ford brought it back from the dead. This time around, it was simply called the GT because, after redesigning the car to increase headroom, the roof was no longer its trademark 40-inches from the tarmac. However, the GT's shark-like nosecone and powerful rear haunches are almost identical to those of the GT40, and it's supercharged 5.4-litre V8 is even more powerful than the original's 4.7-litre motor, capable of pushing it to 200mph and even beyond.

Statistics

Price	£121,000
0-60mph:	3.9sec
0-100mph:	8.6sec
Max speed:	206mph (330kph)
Engine type:	8 cylinders in a V, supercharged
Engine capacity:	5409cc
Bore x stroke:	90.2mm x 105.8mm
Max power:	550bhp @ 6000rpm
Max torque:	500lb ft @ 4500rpm
Power to weight ratio:	347bhp per tonne
Transmission:	six-speed manual gearbox, rear-wheel drive
Kerb weight:	1585kg
Length:	4643mm
Width:	1953mm
Height:	1125mm
Fuel consumption:	12.3mpg
Year introduced:	2004

Ford Mustang Shelby
Cobra GT500

One seriously powerful pony

Ford Mustang Shelby
Cobra GT500

One seriously powerful pony

The Ford Mustang is a car with a history of delivering lots of power for little money; that's what this car, named after a type of wild horse living in America's mid-west, has been doing since its introduction in 1964. None has packed in quite as much horsepower as this one, though – the new Shelby Cobra GT500. Carroll Shelby, the man responsible for the AC Cobra (page 8), originally produced a series of factory-tuned Mustangs in the late 60s, but the GT500, released this year, will be the fastest Mustang he's ever put his name to. Developed by Ford's Special Vehicles Team, the new GT500 features a 450bhp supercharged V8 engine, beefed-up brakes, an upgraded chassis and towering 19in alloy wheels. It'll also be set apart in the same way as the original 60s Shelby Mustangs – by stripes running across the bonnet, roof and boot, from nose to tail.

Statistics

Price	£38,000
0-60mph:	4.5sec*
0-100mph:	10.0sec*
Max speed:	172mph (275kph)*
Engine type:	8 cylinders in a V, supercharged
Engine capacity:	5409cc
Bore x stroke:	90.2mm x 105.8mm
Max power:	450bhp @ 6000rpm
Max torque:	450lb ft @ 4500rpm
Power to weight ratio:	253bhp per tonne
Transmission:	six-speed manual gearbox, rear-wheel drive
Kerb weight:	1780kg
Length:	4775mm
Width:	1877mm
Height:	1384mm
Fuel consumption:	18mpg*
Year introduced:	2006

* figures are estimates

Honda
NSX-R

The ultimate everyday supercar

Honda
NSX-R
The ultimate everyday supercar

People will put up with all manner of compromises to drive a supercar. 'It doesn't matter,' they say, 'that the car of your dreams has a tiny boot and a cramped cabin, that it only does twelve miles per gallon, and that it's harder to get out of than a Hulk Hogan headlock. It's still the car of your dreams.' And they're right. But what if I could tell you that there was a supercar at once spine-tinglingly thrilling and practical. It's the Honda NSX. This is the most thrilling NSX Honda ever made – the Type-R. A standard NSX has power steering, central locking and 276 horsepower; the Type-R has the same 276bhp, but no power steering, no central locking, and carbon fibre where once there was aluminium, making it 145kg lighter. It's almost a second faster to 60mph than a standard NSX, and goes on to 172mph. And yet it's also a Honda, so it'll never break down, it's got room for shopping, and it'll do 23mpg. Brilliant.

Statistics

Price	£75,000
0-60mph:	4.8sec
0-100mph:	10.6sec
Max speed:	173mph (277kph)
Engine type:	6 cylinders in a V
Engine capacity:	3179cc
Bore x stroke:	93mm x 78mm
Max power:	276bhp @ 7300rpm
Max torque:	224lb ft @ 5300rpm
Power to weight ratio:	217bhp per tonne
Transmission:	six-speed manual gearbox, rear-wheel drive
Kerb weight:	1270kg
Length:	4430mm
Width:	1810mm
Height:	1160mm
Fuel consumption:	23mpg
Year introduced:	2002

Jaguar
XJ220

King for 413 days

Jaguar
XJ220

King for 413 days

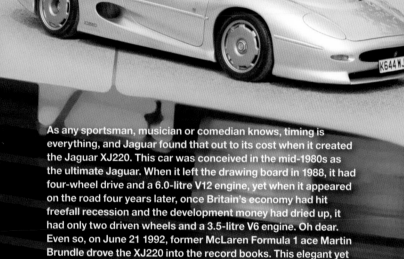

As any sportsman, musician or comedian knows, timing is everything, and Jaguar found that out to its cost when it created the Jaguar XJ220. This car was conceived in the mid-1980s as the ultimate Jaguar. When it left the drawing board in 1988, it had four-wheel drive and a 6.0-litre V12 engine, yet when it appeared on the road four years later, once Britain's economy had hit freefall recession and the development money had dried up, it had only two driven wheels and a 3.5-litre V6 engine. Oh dear. Even so, on June 21 1992, former McLaren Formula 1 ace Martin Brundle drove the XJ220 into the record books. This elegant yet devastatingly fast supercar recorded an incredible 217mph at the Nardo test circuit in Italy, a record that would stand until another British supercar, the McLaren F1, visited the famous five-mile bowl just over a year later. Jaguar had done it; the XJ220, if only for 413 days, was the fastest supercar in history. And what a stunner.

Statistics

Price	£403,000
0-60mph:	3.8sec
0-100mph:	7.3sec
Max speed:	217mph (349kph)
Engine type:	6 cylinders in a V, twin-turbocharged
Engine capacity:	3494cc
Bore x stroke:	94mm x 84mm
Max power:	542bhp @ 7000rpm
Max torque:	475lb ft @ 4500rpm
Power to weight ratio:	395bhp per tonne
Transmission:	five-speed manual gearbox, rear-wheel drive
Kerb weight:	1372kg
Length:	4930mm
Width:	2220mm
Height:	1150mm
Fuel consumption:	13.8mpg
Year introduced:	1992

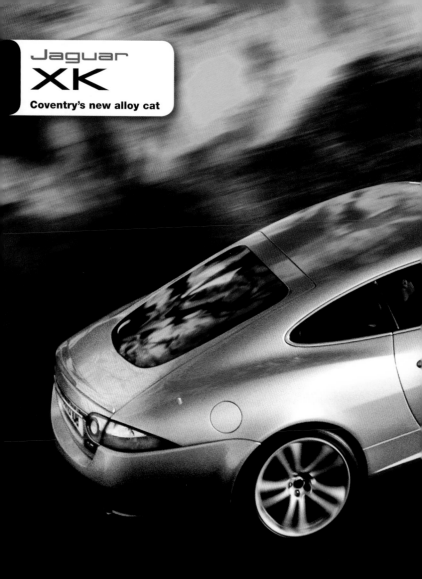

Jaguar
XK

Coventry's new alloy cat

Jaguar
XK
Coventry's new alloy cat

How do you replace the irreplaceable? That's a question that Jaguar's bosses have been pondering ever since the spectacularly beautiful E-type bowed out of production in 1974. Certainly not with the awkward-looking XJS, nor the uninspiring XK8 that came next. However, they may have just found the answer in the shape of a lightweight, agile, good-looking sports car worthy of the E-type's mantle; the new Jaguar XK. This car's design is at once modern and traditional; in the middle of its front bumper is the E-type's instantly-recognisable oval mouth, and further back are muscular-looking haunches and curves. Underneath those curves, however, lurks its real secret; the XK's structure is made up entirely of bonded aluminium, making it 30 per cent stronger than the old XK8, but also 90kg lighter. Here, at last, is a Jaguar that's beautiful and light on its feet, and that drives just as well as it looks.

Statistics

Price	£58,995
0-60mph:	6.0sec
0-100mph:	15.0sec
Max speed:	147mph (235kph)
Engine type:	8 cylinders in a V
Engine capacity:	4196cc
Bore x stroke:	86mm x 90.3mm
Max power:	295bhp @ 6000rpm
Max torque:	310lb ft @ 3500rpm
Power to weight ratio:	185bhp per tonne
Transmission:	six-speed automatic gearbox, rear-wheel drive
Kerb weight:	1595kg
Length:	4791mm
Width:	2065mm
Height:	1322mm
Fuel consumption:	25.0mpg
Year introduced:	2006

Koenigsegg
CCX

Boiled Swede, anyone?

Koenigsegg CCX

Boiled Swede, anyone?

Sweden probably wouldn't be the first place you'd go if you were on a round-the-world shopping spree for supercars. Say you were on the hunt for the ultimate supercar though, there is one Swedish town you should definitely visit: Angelholm – home to Sweden's F10 fighter jet squadron… and to Koenigsegg. You may not have heard of it, but this is a company with twelve years of history, and this year it has unveiled its fastest offering yet – the CCX. Powered by Koenigsegg's own 4.7-litre twin supercharged V8 engine, this is a supercar with some 806bhp, and made of a mixture of plastic and reinforced carbon fibre, it weights only 1180kg. That makes it almost as light as a McLaren F1, but gives it a better power-to-weight ratio than Bugatti's all-conquering Veyron, which it could potentially out-pace when the two high-speed heavyweights eventually go head-to-head. Thought Sweden was only famous for snow, Saabs and Smorgasbord? Then think again.

Statistics

Price	£412,000
0-60mph:	3.2sec
0-100mph:	7.0sec*
Max speed:	246mph (395kph*)
Engine type:	8 cylinders in a V, twin-supercharged
Engine capacity:	4700cc
Bore x stroke:	90mm x 90.3mm
Max power:	806bhp @ 6900rpm
Max torque:	678lb ft @ 5700rpm
Power to weight ratio:	683bhp per tonne
Transmission:	six-speed manual gearbox, rear-wheel drive
Kerb weight:	1180kg
Length:	4293mm
Width:	1996mm
Height:	1120mm
Fuel consumption:	15.5mpg
Year introduced:	2006

* figures have yet to be proved

Lamborghini
Countach

Still in your face at thirty-five

Lamborghini
Countach

Still in your face at thirty-five

There's no direct English translation for the name of this, possibly the most outrageous supercar ever. 'Countach!' was simply what the Italian factory workers who were to build it said upon first clapping eyes on this car. Had it been made in England, it might have been called the 'Crikey', 'Wow' or even the 'Eckey-Thump'. Thankfully though, the Countach was a Lamborghini – the most iconic Lambo of them all. You'll be amazed the first time a Countach rumbles to a stop next to you and the gigantic scissor door pivots upwards and open. It was designed by Bertone's Marcello Gandini, who, being fairly inexperienced at the end of the 1960s, decided to use wedge-shapes rather than curves to characterise the look of the car. The results staggered the supercar world, and the Countach went on to become a movie star and a cultural icon of the 1970s and 80s. There hasn't been another supercar that captured imaginations so powerfully since then, in fact; and that's just when it's stationary.

Statistics

Price	£49,500
0-60mph:	5.6sec
0-100mph:	12.9sec
Max speed:	166mph (266kph)
Engine type:	12 cylinders in a V
Engine capacity:	4754cc
Bore x stroke:	85.5mm x 69.0mm
Max power:	375bhp @ 7000rpm
Max torque:	302lb ft @ 4500rpm
Power to weight ratio:	284bhp per tonne
Transmission:	five-speed manual gearbox, rear-wheel drive
Kerb weight:	1321kg
Length:	4140mm
Width:	2000mm
Height:	1070mm
Fuel consumption:	14.6mpg
Year introduced:	1982

figures apply to LP500 model

Lamborghini
Miura P400S

A prophet in an Italian suit

Lamborghini
Miura P400S

A prophet in an Italian suit

Imagine spending £11,000 (enough, in 1970, for a three-bedroom house in the south of England) on a brand new Lamborghini, travelling to Italy to collect it, levering up the bonnet for a first look at its V12 engine – and finding nothing inside but a spare wheel. How many owners of the Lamborghini Miura do you think demanded their money back on first inspection, convinced their pride and joy was 4.0-litres and twelve cylinders short of finished? Perhaps there was a man specially employed at Sant'Agata to direct angry customers to the Miura's hind-quarters, where the aforementioned engine could be found. There should have been, because the Miura was the world's first mid-engined supercar and, for many, a breed apart all by itself. In 1966 it broke the mould for high-performance cars, not only because its engine was behind the cabin rather than in front of it, but also because it was Lamborghini's most beautiful and desirable creation yet, and its gift to the automotive world was the proof that high speed and effortless beauty could go hand-in-hand.

Price	£10,860
0-60mph:	6.7sec
0-100mph:	15.1sec
Max speed:	173mph (278kph)
Engine type:	12 cylinders in a V
Engine capacity:	3929cc
Bore x stroke:	82.0mm x 62.0mm
Max power:	370bhp @ 7700rpm
Max torque:	286lb ft @ 5500rpm
Power to weight ratio:	285bhp per tonne
Transmission:	five-speed manual gearbox, rear-wheel drive
Kerb weight:	1300kg
Length:	4360mm
Width:	1800mm
Height:	1070mm
Fuel consumption:	14.0mpg
Year introduced:	1970

Lamborghini Murcielago
LP640
Lambo's next big thing

Lamborghini Murcielago
LP640

Lambo's next big thing

It's amazing to think that the V12 engine in this, the latest version of Lamborghini's current Murcielago, started its life more than 40 years ago in the Lambo's very first production car – the 350GT. Back then, the narrow-angle V12 had a comparatively modest 3.5-litre capacity and produced only 280bhp. This year, after almost countless revisions and enlargements, it will have grown to 6.5-litres, and will serve up no less than 640 horsepower. It will feature in the most powerful Lambo ever to charge off the manufacturer's Sant'Agata production line – the Murcielago LP640. The initials 'LP' stand for 'Longitudinale Posteriore', which describes the engine positioning, which is longways (with the cylinder banks running front to rear rather than across the car) and behind the driver. That engine being more powerful than ever, and coupled to a new gearbox, makes this Murcielago scrabble to 62mph in just 3.4sec – 0.4sec faster than a standard one. It should be on sale in the UK this summer, and it'll definitely be one to keep an eye out for.

Price	£195,000 approx*
0-60mph:	3.4sec
0-100mph:	8.2sec*
Max speed:	211mph (338kph)*
Engine type:	12 cylinders in a V
Engine capacity:	6496cc
Bore x stroke:	tbc*
Max power:	640bhp @ 8000rpm
Max torque:	487lb ft @ 6000rpm
Power to weight ratio:	381bhp per tonne
Transmission:	six-speed manual gearbox, four-wheel drive
Kerb weight:	1680kg*
Length:	4610mm
Width:	2058mm
Height:	1135mm
Fuel consumption:	16.0mpg
Year introduced:	2006

* figures have yet to be announced

Lexus
GS450h

The future of the fast four-door

Lexus
GS450h
The future of the fast four-door

Everybody knows that hybrid-electric cars like the Toyota Prius may very well save the world. By storing the energy that's normally wasted when you're driving along and using it to save fuel, they use less of the world's precious natural resources, while coughing out less pollution too. Did you know, however, that hybrid cars could be just as fast as they are environmentally friendly? You're looking at the future of the fast saloon car – it's Lexus' new GS450h. This is a V6-powered saloon car that can crack 60mph in less than six seconds; that's quicker than many of the other supercars on these pages. It's also more than 30 per cent more economical than a typical V8-powered petrol super saloon, and pumps out 80 per cent less CO_2. It's like a BMW M5 that's no harder on the climate than a Ford Mondeo. If all performance cars were this clever, all those mean, green anti-car protesters would be out of a job.

Statistics

Price	**£38,015**
0-60mph:	**5.9sec**
0-100mph:	**n/a**
Max speed:	**156mph (250kph)**
Engine type:	**six cylinders in a V, plus an electric motor**
Engine capacity:	**3495cc**
Bore x stroke:	**94.0mm x 83.0mm**
Max power:	**341bhp @ 6400rpm**
Max torque:	**271lb ft @ 4800rpm**
Power to weight ratio:	**183bhp per tonne**
Transmission:	**continuously variable transmission, rear-wheel drive**
Kerb weight:	**1865kg**
Length:	**4825mm**
Width:	**1820mm**
Height:	**1430mm**
Fuel consumption:	**35.8mpg**
Year introduced:	**2006**

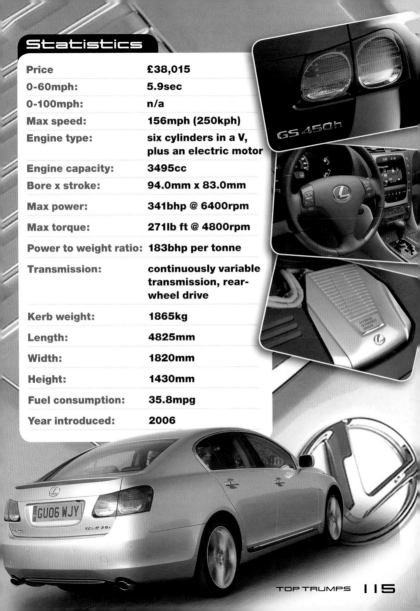

GS 450h

GU06 WJY

Lotus
Esprit V8

The wedge gets added edge

R482 AAH

Lotus
Esprit V8
The wedge gets added edge

The Lotus Esprit suffered from the same lingering problem for much of its life: it looked a lot faster than it actually was. Many Esprit owners who bought their cars in the late 70s and 80s were seduced by its exotic, wedge-shaped looks. They hailed their cars as examples of the finest British mid-engined sports cars of a generation, and rightly so; an Esprit handles, steers and corners with the best of 'em. What it lacked, restricted to a series of small four-cylinder engines, was the power to punch hard enough in a straight line to call itself a real supercar. That was until the Esprit V8 was launched in 1996. In a bid to create a car to go racing with, Lotus designed a twin-turbocharged 3.5-litre V8 engine small enough to fit into the Esprit's engine bay. In road tune, this V8 developed 349bhp, and was strong enough to turn the Esprit, at last, into the Brit-built Ferrari-baiter it should have been from the off.

Price	**£59,995**
0-60mph:	**4.5sec**
0-100mph:	**10.5sec**
Max speed:	**176mph (282kph)**
Engine type:	**Eight cylinders in a V, twin turbocharged**
Engine capacity:	**3506cc**
Bore x stroke:	**81.0mm x 83.0mm**
Max power:	**349bhp @ 6500rpm**
Max torque:	**295lb ft @ 4250rpm**
Power to weight ratio:	**253bhp per tonne**
Transmission:	**five-speed manual, rear-wheel drive**
Kerb weight:	**1380kg**
Length:	**4414mm**
Width:	**1883mm**
Height:	**1150mm**
Fuel consumption:	**21.2mpg**
Year introduced:	**1996**

R482 AAH

Lotus
Exige S

Hethel's one-tonne tearaway

Lotus
Exige S

Hethel's one-tonne tearaway

Though it lacks some of the ingredients of our other collected supercars – ingredients such as a woofling multicylinder engine, jaw-dropping looks, historical significance or a seven figure price tag – you should definitely not overlook the Lotus Exige S. With a supercharged and furious 1.8-litre engine mounted directly behind the driver's head, incredible levels of grip, pin-sharp handling and a kerbweight so low that most city cars struggle to match it, this little firecracker screams to be taken very seriously indeed. The Exige S represents everything that's great about Lotus too. In turning this Elise-based track car into a car capable of exchanging blows with a Porsche Cayman S, Lotus could have elected to make it bigger, and cram in a larger six- or eight-cylinder engine. Instead it stayed true to the values of compactness and agility that have made its cars so thrilling to drive, and in adding a supercharger to the Exige's already-heady mix, gave it more power-per-kilogram of kerbweight than a Ferrari 348.

Statistics

Price	£33,995
0-60mph:	4.1sec
0-100mph:	10.5sec
Max speed:	148mph (238kph)
Engine type:	Four cylinders in a line, supercharged
Engine capacity:	1796cc
Bore x stroke:	82.0mm x 85.0mm
Max power:	218bhp @ 7800rpm
Max torque:	159lb ft @ 5500rpm
Power to weight ratio:	233bhp per tonne
Transmission:	six-speed manual, rear-wheel drive
Kerb weight:	935kg
Length:	3797mm
Width:	1727mm
Height:	1159mm
Fuel consumption:	31.0mpg
Year introduced:	2005

Maserati
Bora

The forgotten supercar

Maserati
Bora

The forgotten supercar

Few pleasures are more satisfying than knowing something your neighbour doesn't. Appreciating the Maserati Bora provides that kind of satisfaction. It's the forgotten supercar; a mid-engined two-seater, the Bora was beaten to market by the Lamborghini Miura and overshadowed by the Ferrari Dino. Despite all that, though, the Bora was undoubtedly one of the finest mid-engined supercars of its generation. You only have to flick back a few pages to discover that this little-known Maserati was half a second faster to 60mph than the Miura, and had superb brakes and steering to match. It was far-and-away the most practical car of its kind too, with room for two sets of golf clubs on top of the engine cover, and extra room in the front for bags. When Maserati was bought out by De Tomaso in the late 1970s, the Bora faded into obscurity, and now that the company is twinned with Ferrari, we'll probably never see its like again. All the more reason to remember the Bora, then; a car from a time when Maserati used to take on the Italian heavyweights – and win.

Statistics

Price	£9860
0-60mph:	6.2sec
0-100mph:	13.4sec
Max speed:	168mph (270kph)
Engine type:	Eight cylinders in a V
Engine capacity:	4719cc
Bore x stroke:	93.9mm x 85.0mm
Max power:	310bhp @ 6000rpm
Max torque:	325lb ft @ 4200rpm
Power to weight ratio:	204bhp per tonne
Transmission:	five-speed manual, rear-wheel drive
Kerb weight:	1520kg
Length:	4335mm
Width:	1768mm
Height:	1138mm
Fuel consumption:	12mpg
Year introduced:	1971

Maserati
Quattroporte

Like a Ferrari for all the family

Maserati
Quattroport■

Like a Ferrari for all the family

Practicality isn't a Ferrari forte; it has yet to produce a family car with four seats, four doors, a decent-sized boot and the same jaw-on-the-floor looks, speed and driver appeal that runs throughout its range of exotic spyders and coupés. Thankfully, its sister company Maserati has produced such a car; in 2004, it saw fit to unleash a saloon car with a generous dose of Latin supercar spirit onto the market – the Quattroporte. The Quattroporte (which means 'four door' in Italian) is the kind of car you'd expect the heads of Italian industry to drive. Its elegant curves come from the sketchbooks of Pininfarina, the styling specialist famed for having drawn so many Italian supercars, and clothe a car with sufficient comfort and cabin room for four finely-tailored Mafia bosses. With a glorious-sounding 400bhp V8 to call upon, it's also got the power to eventually outpace a BMW M5 on the autostrada, and surprisingly impressive cornering capabilities when the going gets twisty too.

Price	£74,595
0-60mph:	5.3sec
0-100mph:	12.8sec
Max speed:	162mph (259kph)
Engine type:	Eight cylinders in a V
Engine capacity:	4244cc
Bore x stroke:	92.0mm x 79.8mm
Max power:	400bhp @ 7000rpm
Max torque:	333lb ft @ 4500rpm
Power to weight ratio:	207bhp per tonne
Transmission:	six-speed manual, rear-wheel drive
Kerb weight:	1930kg
Length:	5052mm
Width:	1895mm
Height:	1438mm
Fuel consumption:	14.9mpg
Year introduced:	2004

McLaren
F1

Top of the pile

McLaren F1

Top of the pile

For longer than a decade the McLaren F1 stood as the embodiment of the word fast. Born out of a wish by Formula 1 team McLaren to make the ultimate performance car, the very best design and engineering prowess, the most advanced components, and the best materials money could buy were lavished on it. That's why, if you lift the engine bay, you'll find a lining of gold plating worthy of a coronation, because gold reflects heat better than any other metal. This incredible supercar hit 231mph in 1993, dismissing the claims of the Jaguar XJ220 and Bugatti EB110 as the fastest production car ever. In 1998, it was driven to 240.1mph, a figure that the Ferrari Enzo couldn't get close to. Even now, the likes of the Bugatti Veyron and Koenigsegg CCX have still to independently prove that they will go faster; the F1's place in history, on the other hand, is assured. Perhaps it's no longer the very fastest road car ever made, yet it remains the crowning automotive achievement.

Statistics

Price	£540,000
0-60mph:	3.2sec
0-100mph:	6.3sec
Max speed:	240mph (386kph)
Engine type:	Twelve cylinders in a V
Engine capacity:	6064cc
Bore x stroke:	86mm x 87mm
Max power:	627bhp @ 7400rpm
Max torque:	479lb ft @ 4000rpm
Power to weight ratio:	550bhp per tonne
Transmission:	six-speed manual, rear-wheel drive
Kerb weight:	1138kg
Length:	4288mm
Width:	1820mm
Height:	1140mm
Fuel consumption:	15.2mpg
Year introduced:	1994

Mercedes
R63 AMG

Hold on in the back row

S:FA 7194

Mercedes
R63 AMG

Hold on in the back row

Most of the supercars you've been reading about in this book have
the same recognisable make-up; you could call it supercar DNA.
Mainly, they're as compact, as light and as low to the ground as
possible, they have two seats, two driven wheels, and as powerful
an engine as you can conceive of; that's why they're so fast. The
question is, why shouldn't you have a supercar that's the size of a big
estate car? Why shouldn't a supercar have room for six people and
have four-wheel drive to deal with slippery conditions? Can you think
of a good reason? Neither can Mercedes – that's why it's launched
this, the R63 AMG. Like any other R-class, the R63's got six seats
as roomy as you'll find in most luxury saloons, and four-wheel drive
– but it's also got 503bhp, which is enough to catapult it, you and five
of your friends, to 62mph in exactly five seconds. It's the first ever
super-people-mover.

Statistics

Price	£69,995*
0-60mph:	5.0sec
0-100mph:	11.5sec*
Max speed:	156mph (250kph)
Engine type:	8 cylinders in a V
Engine capacity:	6208cc
Bore x stroke:	102.2mm x 94.2mm
Max power:	503bhp @ 6800rpm
Max torque:	465lb ft @ 5200rpm
Power to weight ratio:	224bhp per tonne
Transmission:	seven-speed automatic gearbox, four-wheel drive
Kerb weight:	2250kg*
Length:	4925mm
Width:	1922mm
Height:	1659mm
Fuel consumption:	17mpg*
Year introduced:	2006

* figures are estimates,
as they're as yet unreleased

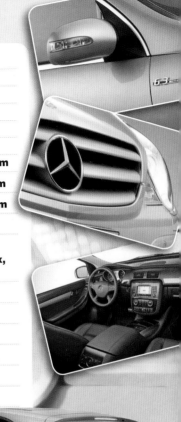

Mercedes SLR
McLaren

Sounds like trouble

Mercedes SLR
McLaren

Sounds like trouble

It's the sound that the Mercedes SLR McLaren makes that'll get you. Not the way it looks, because being capable of 207mph, you probably won't see it for very long. Should one of these fantastic Mercedes supercars rocket past in the outside lane, the only way you'll know about it is the lingering and aggressive 'chugga-chugga-chug' emanating from those huge, sideways-facing exhausts. Remember the noise that Sebulba's pod racer made in *Star Wars: Epidose 1*? Well, the SLR makes the same kind of deep, guttural throb you feel in the pit of your stomach. At full throttle, it makes you want to run away and hide. The noise it makes, however, is just one of many factors making the SLR one of the most evocative supercars on the road. Although made by the same company that built your mum's A-class, it's faster than a Lamborghini Diablo, and yet, with a five-speed fully-automatic gearbox, it's as usable as most family hatchbacks.

Statistics

Price	£313,565
0-60mph:	3.8sec
0-100mph:	7.6sec
Max speed:	207mph (333kph)
Engine type:	Eight cylinders in a V, supercharged
Engine capacity:	5439cc
Bore x stroke:	97mm x 92mm
Max power:	626bhp @ 6500rpmm
Max torque:	575lb ft @ 5000rpm
Power to weight ratio:	370bhp per tonne
Transmission:	five-speed automatic, rear-wheel drive
Kerb weight:	1693kg
Length:	4656mm
Width:	1908mm
Height:	1261mm
Fuel consumption:	19.5mpg
Year introduced:	2003

Mitsubishi Evo
VIII MR-FQ400

McRae's worst nightmare

Mitsubishi Evo
VIII MR-FQ400

McRae's worst nightmare

Colin McRae isn't just a name on a Playstation game; some say he was the most talented rally driver the world has ever seen. But McRae only ever won the World Rally Championship once, in 1995; he was beaten to the title in '96, '97, '98 and '99 by the same man, driving the same car. The man? Flying Finn Tommi Makinen… and the car? The Mitsubishi Lancer Evolution. This four-wheel drive, turbocharged four-door dominated world rallying in the late 1990s, making a reputation for itself as the fastest car in creation across mud, snow, gravel and ice. It was no surprise that so many drivers wanted an Evo of their own to tear up the road in, but it wasn't until 2004 that they were given the ultimate road-going Evo – the FQ400. Most Evos have between 270 and 300 horsepower; this one has over 400. It's faster to 60mph than a Ferrari F40, and while most supercars flounder in slippery conditions, this one just powerslides on through them.

Statistics

Price	£46,999
0-60mph:	3.5sec
0-100mph:	9.1sec
Max speed:	176mph (282kph)
Engine type:	4 cylinders in a line, turbocharged
Engine capacity:	1997cc
Bore x stroke:	85mm x 88mm
Max power:	405bhp @ 6400rpm
Max torque:	355lb ft @ 5500rpm
Power to weight ratio:	287bhp per tonne
Transmission:	six-speed manual gearbox, four-wheel drive
Kerb weight:	1410kg
Length:	4490mm
Width:	1770mm
Height:	1450mm
Fuel consumption:	18mpg
Year introduced:	2004

Nissan Skyline
GT-R Z-Tune

An eastern legend's parting shot

ssan Skyline
GT-R Z-Tune

astern legend's parting shot

t'd be wrong to work our way through this catalogue of the most fantastic cars in the world without stopping to consider the greatest one ever to come out of Japan – the Skyline GT-R, beloved of millions of gamers the world over. Like so many of Japan's exports, the Skyline's trump card is technological genius. It's not only wickedly powerful, but thanks to an army of computers, it can deploy that power onto the tarmac through whichever set of wheels has the most grip. It even steers with all four wheels. The Skyline GT-R was introduced in 1989. It has been through three model generations since then, and each has proved its credentials by setting the fastest laptime of any production car around Germany's legendary 14-mile Nürburgring circuit. It's a very fast car indeed. The GT-R Z-Tune, the very last GT-R, features an enlarged and derestricted 2.8-litre twin-turbocharged engine, a racing chassis and bucket seats. It's easily the most monstrous Skyline of them all, and that, as they say, is saving something.

Statistics

Price	**£84,500**
0-60mph:	**3.5sec***
0-100mph:	**8.5sec***
Max speed:	**201mph (322kph)***
Engine type:	**Six cylinders in a line, twin turbocharged**
Engine capacity:	**2771cc**
Bore x stroke:	**87.9mm x 77.7mm**
Max power:	**493bhp @ 6800rpm**
Max torque:	**398lb ft @ 5200rpm**
Power to weight ratio:	**308bhp per tonne**
Transmission:	**six-speed manual gearbox, four-wheel drive**
Kerb weight:	**1600kg**
Length:	**4600mm**
Width:	**1785mm**
Height:	**1360mm**
Fuel consumption:	**16mpg***
Year introduced:	**2005**

* figures are estimates; information is undisclosed

Noble
M400
Britain's supercar killer

Noble
M400
Britain's supercar killer

What if someone organised a tournament for the world's fastest cars – a kind of world cup for supercars, open to all cars still in production anywhere in the world. Say this contest covered all disciplines a supercar should excel in; acceleration, braking, cornering and maximum speed. Which car do you think Britain should send? Can't have the McLaren F1; they don't make it anymore. Aston Martin Vanquish S, perhaps? Not quick enough off the mark. What about an Ariel Atom then? Not quick enough above 100mph. What we'd need would be the perfect all-rounder – a kind of four-wheeled Steven Gerrard. Step forward the Noble M400. So called because of its massive 400bhp per tonne, the M400 is Britain's current performance king. It's fast enough in a straight line to keep up with most 550bhp supercars, and yet because it's so light, will corner quicker than almost anything else on the track. Want to fly the flag for Britain from your chosen supercar? Then this Noble beast is definitely for you.

Statistics

Price	**£55,995**
0-60mph:	**3.5sec**
0-100mph:	**8.8sec**
Max speed:	**185mph (297kph)**
Engine type:	**Six cylinders in a V, twin turbocharged**
Engine capacity:	**2968cc**
Bore x stroke:	**89.0mm x 79.5mm**
Max power:	**425bhp @ 6500rpm**
Max torque:	**390lb ft @ 5000rpm**
Power to weight ratio:	**401bhp per tonne**
Transmission:	**six-speed manual gearbox, rear-wheel drive**
Kerb weight:	**1060kg**
Length:	**4089mm**
Width:	**1828mm**
Height:	**1143mm**
Fuel consumption:	**18mpg**
Year introduced:	**2004**

Pagani Zonda C12F
Clubsport

Italy's newest supercar

Pagani Zonda C12F
Clubsport

Italy's newest supercar

Pagani is a supercar company that, like Koenigsegg, has come
from relative obscurity to hero status in the space of just a few
years. At the beginning of the 1990s, Horacio Pagani was just an
Italian businessman who made carbon fibre parts for the supercar
industry. Then, in 1999, he unveiled his own supercar to the
world – the Zonda C12. In the space of just seven years, through
refinement and overhaul, the Zonda has become one of the most
revered supercars in the world. The latest model is faster than
a Porsche Carrera GT, and could go head-to-head with a Ferrari
Enzo without fear of embarrassment. In other words, Pagani has
scalped the supercar establishment in less time than it takes most
manufacturers to engineer a family hatchback. This is his latest
and most powerful Zonda, the C12F Clubsport – elegant, stunningly
beautiful, and built with circuit racing in mind.

Statistics

Price	£450,000
0-60mph:	3.5sec
0-100mph:	7.2sec
Max speed:	215mph (344kph)
Engine type:	Twelve cylinders in a V
Engine capacity:	7291cc
Bore x stroke:	91.5mm x 92.4mm
Max power:	650bhp @ 6200rpm
Max torque:	575lb ft @ 4000rpm
Power to weight ratio:	528bhp per tonne
Transmission:	six-speed manual gearbox, rear-wheel drive
Kerb weight:	1230kg
Length:	4435mm
Width:	2055mm
Height:	1141mm
Fuel consumption:	16mpg
Year introduced:	2006

Pontiac GTO

The original muscle car

Pontiac
GTO
The original muscle car

Some world firsts are better known than others. First man on the moon? That's an easy one (Neil Armstrong). First supercar to crack 200mph? That's a bit more difficult (the Ferrari F40). What about the first in America's long line of muscle cars? Allow me to introduce it – the Pontiac GTO. The term muscle car can apply to any car implanted with a larger engine than its size or weight requires. Historically though, it refers to a particular group of American performance cars to which the Chevrolet Camaro, Dodge Charger and Pontiac Firebird belong – all average-sized cars with outsized engines. The GTO was the first, arriving in 1964. If you stripped it down, the GTO was just a Pontiac Tempest (which ordinarily got a 5.3-litre V8) fitted with wider wheels, stiffer springs, bonnet scoops and a 6.4-litre motor from a Pontiac Catalina. That bigger engine gave it the power to rocket to 60mph in just 6.6 seconds though, and its spirit lives on in every performance saloon and coupé on the road today.

Statistics

Price	£1600
0-60mph:	6.6sec
0-100mph:	15.0sec
Max speed:	165mph (265kph)
Engine type:	Eight cylinders in a V
Engine capacity:	6376cc
Bore x stroke:	103.1mm x 95.3mm
Max power:	348bhp @ 4900rpm
Max torque:	428lb ft @ 3600rpm
Power to weight ratio:	219bhp per tonne
Transmission:	four-speed manual gearbox, rear-wheel drive
Kerb weight:	1588kg
Length:	5242mm
Width:	1890mm
Height:	1372mm
Fuel consumption:	12mpg
Year introduced:	1964

Porsche 911
GT3 RS

The naughtiest 42-year-old on the block

Porsche 911
GT3 RS

The naughtiest 42-year-old on the block

If you don't recognise it by the huge decals on its flanks, then you'll definitely clock the gigantic rear spoiler of Porsche's most specialised 911 ever – the GT3 RS. The 911's history flows all the way back to 1964, and emerging from it at the top of any particular pile is no small achievement. However, if you could only pick one 911 – the one to thrill your senses and frazzle your brain more than any other – you'd pick this one. There are faster 911s, so what makes this one so great? In one word, drama. There isn't another 911, and few other supercars, that bombard you with so much sensation; the RS's engine is a spluttering, raucous masterpiece, its steering so accurate you could guide missiles with it, and its chassis so stiff that it only really comes into its own at the track. You need to push this car as hard as you dare to get the best out of it, but if you do, nothing will put a broader smile on your face.

Statistics

Price	**£84,230**
0-60mph:	**4.4sec**
0-100mph:	**9.7sec**
Max speed:	**191mph (306kph)**
Engine type:	**Six cylinders horizontally opposed**
Engine capacity:	**3600cc**
Bore x stroke:	**100mm x 76mm**
Max power:	**381bhp @ 7300rpm**
Max torque:	**284lb ft @ 5000rpm**
Power to weight ratio:	**282bhp per tonne**
Transmission:	**six-speed manual gearbox, rear-wheel drive**
Kerb weight:	**1350kg**
Length:	**4435mm**
Width:	**1950mm**
Height:	**1350mm**
Fuel consumption:	**19.7mpg**
Year introduced:	**2003**

Porsche
959

All-wheel drive pioneer

Porsche
959
All-wheel drive pioneer

If you remember the Porsche 959 at all (and there are plenty of us who do), you'll probably remember it for one reason. This was the supercar that fell short of breaking the 200mph barrier by a piffling three miles per hour. If it had been ever-so-slightly sleeker, lighter or more powerful, anyone who cares even a little bit about cars would probably remember it. But never mind that; the reason we should recognise the 959 as an all time great is because without it Porsche's longest-running and most famous sports car, the 911, would almost certainly be dead. The 959 was the testbed for the four-wheel drive system that, later on, would literally keep the 911 on the road, and in production. It was an amazingly good-looking, amenable and safe-handling supercar too, and, clocking 197mph, hardly slow. Just as some supercars blaze their own name across the sky though, others serve as technological pioneers. In other words, the 959 was a real hero's car – you just never knew it.

Price	**£150,000**
0-60mph:	**3.7sec**
0-100mph:	**8.5sec**
Max speed:	**197mph (317kph)**
Engine type:	**Six cylinders horizontally opposed, twin turbocharged**
Engine capacity:	**2849cc**
Bore x stroke:	**95mm x 67mm**
Max power:	**450bhp @ 6500rpm**
Max torque:	**370lb ft @ 5500rpm**
Power to weight ratio:	**339bhp per tonne**
Transmission:	**six-speed manual gearbox, four-wheel drive**
Kerb weight:	**1323kg**
Length:	**4260mm**
Width:	**1839mm**
Height:	**1280mm**
Fuel consumption:	**14mpg**
Year introduced:	**1986**

BB·PW 287

Porsche
Carrera GT

Not just another Porsche

Carrera GT

Porsche
Carrera GT
Not just another Porsche

This is the latest and greatest Porsche to roll out of the company's factory in Leipzig, Germany – the 603bhp, 205mph, £321,000 Carrera GT. It was an important car for Porsche; a supercar from a company known mainly for its sports cars and its race cars. Critics of Porsche would say that it shouldn't have made it; that the calm engineering excellence and deliberate precision that Porsche has built a reputation on don't add up to building compelling supercars. After all, could a Porsche ever strike you dumb in the same way that a Lamborghini or Ferrari could? If the 959 left a tiny margin of doubt in that department, the Carrera GT certainly didn't. Here is a car with everything that it takes to blow you away in epic style. Staggeringly gorgeous, unrepentantly noisy, addictively fast and yet still so easy to drive, the Carrera GT is one of the most exciting supercars ever made.

Statistics

Price	**£321,000**
0-60mph:	**3.7sec**
0-100mph:	**7.4sec**
Max speed:	**205mph (330kph)**
Engine type:	**Ten cylinders in a V**
Engine capacity:	**5733cc**
Bore x stroke:	**98mm x 76mm**
Max power:	**603bhp @ 8000rpm**
Max torque:	**435lb ft @ 5750rpm**
Power to weight ratio:	**410bhp per tonne**
Transmission:	**six-speed manual gearbox, rear-wheel drive**
Kerb weight:	**1472kg**
Length:	**4613mm**
Width:	**1921mm**
Height:	**1166mm**
Fuel consumption:	**15.2mpg**
Year introduced:	**2004**

Subaru
Impreza 22B

A rally-bred collector's item

Subaru
Impreza 22B

A rally-bred collector's item

Wouldn't it be great if you could buy Michael Schumacher's
Ferrari F1 car just hours after he'd finished the British Grand Prix
in it? Unfortunately, Ferrari guards its F1 cars very carefully, and
even if you could buy one, you'd be breaking almost every law in
the book by driving an F1 car on the road. However, when Subaru
launched the Impreza 22B in 1998, it gave us the next best thing
– the chance to buy Colin McRae's World Rally Car in just-about-
road-legal form. The 22B is so close to the specification of the
Impreza WRC car that it might as well have '555' stickers on
each flank; it's got the flared wheel arches, gigantic disc brakes,
a fitted roll cage – even an adjustable rear spoiler and Subaru's
trick centre differential. Only 400 were made, and most sold out
within 24 hours of release. For those select few though, this was
the last word in WRC cool.

Price	**£40,000**
0-60mph:	**4.4sec**
0-100mph:	**11.0sec**
Max speed:	**112mph (180kph)**
Engine type:	**Four cylinders horizontally opposed, turbocharged**
Engine capacity:	**2212cc**
Bore x stroke:	**96.9mm x 75mm**
Max power:	**276bhp @ 6000rpm**
Max torque:	**266lb ft @ 3200rpm**
Power to weight ratio:	**217bhp per tonne**
Transmission:	**five-speed manual gearbox, four-wheel drive**
Kerb weight:	**1267kg**
Length:	**4365mm**
Width:	**1770mm**
Height:	**1390mm**
Fuel consumption:	**21.6mpg**
Year introduced:	**1998**

TVR
Sagaris

Scary mover

Sagaris

TVR
Sagaris

Scary mover

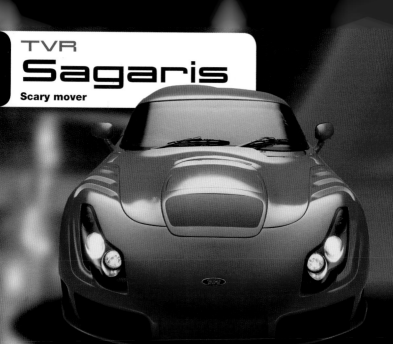

Looks like it's about ready to drive off the page and into a horror movie, doesn't it? That's the TVR Sagaris, designed more than any other supercar to shock, surprise, astound and amaze. However, if you think the savage looks might be a ruse – that the Sagaris might be all show and no go – you'd be wrong. Underneath those sensational vents and bulges lurks a fearsome heart, and if you like your supercars brutally fast and raw, it's one that'll occupy your daydreams more than any other. Blackpool-based TVR is known for having unleashed some fairly unrepentant sports cars upon the world, and the Sagaris is no different. With more than 400 horsepower from its 4.0-litre straight six engine, and weighing not much more than a tonne, this car can hit 60mph in less than four seconds, and keeps going until 185mph. You'll need a supercar of the very fastest kind to escape one – and even then, there's no guarantee that it won't pop up in your nightmares.

Statistics

Price	£49,995
0-60mph:	3.9sec
0-100mph:	8.5sec
Max speed:	185mph (298kph)
Engine type:	Six cylinders in a line
Engine capacity:	3996cc
Bore x stroke:	96.0mm x 92.0mm
Max power:	406bhp @ 7000rpm
Max torque:	349lb ft @ 5000rpm
Power to weight ratio:	377bhp per tonne
Transmission:	five-speed manual gearbox, rear-wheel drive
Kerb weight:	1078kg
Length:	4057mm
Width:	1850mm
Height:	1175mm
Fuel consumption:	15.1mpg
Year introduced:	2005

Volkswagen Golf
R32

Who needs a supercar?

Volkswagen Golf
R32

Who needs a supercar?

Finally, we come to the end of our automotive alphabet;
Volkswagen, and the Golf GTi. The GTi's 30 this year; there's
a decent chance that your dad, your uncle, or your next door
neighbour had one back in the mists of time, and they'll be able
to fill you in on how great a car it was. Here, we'll cut a long story
short; it was the first ever hot hatchback and, some say, the most
enjoyable to drive too. Thirty years ago though, GTis only had
front-wheel drive and 108bhp; today, you can get one with four-
wheel drive and 247bhp – the Golf R32. Right now, this Golf is the
most powerful hatchback on the planet. It'll accelerate to 60mph
in six seconds dead – that's faster than the Lamborghini Miura,
Maserati Bora and the Aston Martin DB4, all supercars you've
already read about. Unlike those supercars though, it's got room
for four people plus some shopping. Now there's a lesson
in progress.

Statistics

Price	**£23,745**
0-60mph:	**6.0sec**
0-100mph:	**15.5sec**
Max speed:	**145mph (233kph)**
Engine type:	**Six cylinders in a V**
Engine capacity:	**3189cc**
Bore x stroke:	**84.0mm x 95.9mm**
Max power:	**247bhp @ 6300rpm**
Max torque:	**236lb ft @ 2800rpm**
Power to weight ratio:	**155bhp per tonne**
Transmission:	**six-speed manual gearbox, four-wheel drive**
Kerb weight:	**1590kg**
Length:	**4246mm**
Width:	**2000mm**
Height:	**1465mm**
Fuel consumption:	**26.2mpg**
Year introduced:	**2005**

Checklist

 AC • Cobra 289
Date   Location

 Ariel • Atom 300
Date   Location

 Aston Martin • DB4 GT Zagato
Date   Location

 Aston Martin • Vanquish S
Date   Location

 Audi • Quattro
Date   Location

 Audi • R8
Date   Location

 Audi • RS4
Date   Location

 BMW • M3 CSL
Date   Location

 BMW • M5
Date   Location

 Brabus • Rocket
Date   Location

Bugatti • Veyron 16.4

Date   **Location**

Caterham • CSR 260

Date   **Location**

Chevrolet • Corvette Z06

Date   **Location**

Ferrari • 250 GTO

Date   **Location**

Ferrari • Enzo

Date   **Location**

Ferrari • F40

Date   **Location**

Ford • Focus RS

Date   **Location**

Ford • GT

Date   **Location**

Ford • Mustang Shelby GT500

Date   **Location**

Honda • NSX-R

Date   **Location**

Jaguar • XJ220

Date   **Location**

Jaguar • XK

Date   Location

Koenigsegg • CCX

Date   Location

Lamborghini • Countach

Date   Location

Lamborghini • Miura

Date   Location

Lamborghini • Murcielago LP640

Date   Location

Lexus • GS450h

Date   Location

Lotus • Esprit V8

Date   Location

Lotus • Exige S

Date   Location

Maserati • Bora

Date   Location

Maserati • Quattroporte

Date   Location

McLaren • F1

Date   Location

Mercedes • R63 AMG

Date   Location

Mercedes • SLR McLaren

Date **Location**

Mitsubishi • Evo VIII MR-FQ400

Date **Location**

Nissan • Skyline GT-R

Date **Location**

Noble • M400

Date **Location**

Pagani • Zonda C12F

Date **Location**

Pontiac • GTO

Date **Location**

Porsche • 911 GT3 RS

Date **Location**

Porsche • 959

Date **Location**

Porsche • Carrera GT

Date **Location**

Subaru • Impreza 22B

Date **Location**

TVR • Sagaris

Date **Location**

Volkswagen • Golf R32

Date **Location**

Look out for the other
Top Trumps Books

www.haynes.co.uk

...and all the
Top Trumps Cards

CLASSICS Dinosaurs • Gumball 3000 Supercars 2 • Predators • Sharks • Skyscrapers • Space Phenomena • The Dog • Ultimate Military Jets • Warships • Wonders of the World

SPECIALS Bratz: Passion for Fashion • DC Super Heroes 1 (Batman) • DC Super Heroes 2 (Superman) • Doctor Who • Harry Potter and the Goblet of Fire • Horror • Jacqueline Wilson • Marvel Comic Heroes 3 • Marvel Comic Villains • Roald Dahl: Goodies & Baddies • Smash Hits Popstars 3 • Star Wars: Episodes I-III • Star Wars: Episodes IV-VI • Star Wars: Starships • The Da Vinci Code • The Chronicles of Narnia 1 • The Simpsons Classic Collection 1

SPORTS Arsenal FC 2007 • Chelsea FC 2007 • Liverpool FC 2007 • Manchester United FC 2007 • Newcastle United FC • World Football Stars • WWE Superstars 1 • WWE Superstars 2

Play Top Trumps at
TOPTRUMPS.COM